TRANSPORT IN
EUROPE

Mark Smalley

Wayland

EUROPE

Energy in Europe
Europe and the Environment
Europe and its History
Farming in Europe
Industry in Europe
Living in Europe
Tourism in Europe
Transport in Europe

Series Editor: Janet De Saulles
Book Editor: Judy Martin
Series Design: Bridgewater Design
Book Design: Jackie Berry

First published in 1991 by Wayland (Publishers) Ltd.,
61, Western Road, Hove, BN3 1JD, England

British Library Cataloguing in Publication Data

Smalley, Mark
Transport in Europe.
I. Title
388.094

ISBN 0 7502 0150 9

Typeset by Dorchester Typesetting Group Ltd.
Printed in Italy by G Canale C.S.p.A., Turin
Bound in France by A.G.M.

ACKNOWLEDGEMENTS

Bridgeman Art Library 7, 8 (bottom); Neil Bruce (Peter Roberts Collection) 8 (top); Commission of the European Communities 14; Eye Ubiquitous (Davy Bold) 13, (Nick Wiseman) 21, (Yiorgos Nikiteas) 22, (Derek Redfearn) 32, (John Read) 33, (Frank Leather) 34 (top), (Geoff Redmayne) 34 (bottom), (Yiorgos Nikiteas) 44 (top) Greenpeace/Berghezan 28 (top); Greenpeace/Boitet 44 (bottom); Tony Stone (Mark Wagner) 3, (David Harding) 4, (Oliver Benn) 6, (David H Endersby) 15, (Bruno de Hogues) 19 (top), (Charles Thatcher) 26, (Alan Bianchi) 27 (top), (Ary Diesendruck) 27 (bottom), (Adrian Neal) 36, (Alan Smith) 40, (Mark Wagner) 41; Topham 11; Zefa 11, 12, 17, 24, 35, 39, 42; Wayland Picture Library 19 (bottom), 28 (bottom), 29, 30, 31, 38. Cover and all interior artwork by Malcolm Walker.

21133520H

Contents

Introduction

Transport is the movement of people or goods from one place to another. This book traces the importance of transport in European life today. People use transport because they need to go somewhere. In their daily lives Europeans travel to school or work. They use transport to go shopping, during leisure-time to visit friends and family, and when going on holiday. We use a wide variety of different forms of transport. Walking and cycling are used for local trips. Private transport, such as the family car, is generally used for longer journeys. Public transport, such as trains, trams or buses, might be used for longer or shorter journeys.

Above **Commuters pouring off the trains at rush hour.**

Transport is essential to the economy. Without it, commercial goods (or freight) could not be traded within and between countries. As lorries, trains, ships and planes have become faster, the world seems to have become a smaller place.

Take this book as an example. What you are now holding in your hands tells us a lot about transport and commerce in Europe. The paper comes from Sweden. The book was printed in Italy and put together in France. It was then transported to shops in Britain before ending up with you.

Right **A map of Europe showing natural boundaries and passes. Rivers such as the Rhine link up a number of European countries and make transport and communication possible.**

ICELAND

SCANDINAVIAN PENINSULA

NORWAY

SWEDEN

FINLAND

USSR

BALTIC SEA

ESTONIA

LATVIA

LITHUANIA

PLAIN

EUROPEAN BYELORUSSIA

SCOTLAND

NORTH SEA

NORTHERN IRELAND

DENMARK

IRELAND

UNITED KINGDOM

ENGLAND

WALES

R. Thames

THE NETHERLANDS

R. Elbe

GREAT

R. Wisla

POLAND

UKRAINE

ATLANTIC OCEAN

BELGIUM

GERMANY

CZECHOSLOVAKIA

Carpathian Mts.

MOLDAVIA

LUX.

R. Seine

R. Rhine

R. Danube

AUSTRIA

HUNGARY

ROMANIA

BLACK SEA

R. Loire

FRANCE

SWITZ.

THE ALPS

Auvergne Mts.

R. Danube

R. Po

Dinaric Alps

YUGOSLAVIA

Balkan Mts.

BULGARIA

R. Garonne

ITALY

Adriatic Sea

Appenines

ALBANIA

Pindus Mts.

Anatolian Plateau

PORTUGAL

PYRENEES

CORSICA

TURKEY

IBERIAN PENINSULA

R. Tagus

SPAIN

Balearic Is.

SARDINIA

SICILY

GREECE

MEDITERRANEAN SEA

MALTA

A boat transports goods through Frankfurt, down the River Maine.

TRANSPORT AND GEOGRAPHY

Europe's physical geography has played its part in shaping the kinds of transport used throughout the continent. Natural features such as rivers, mountains and seas have long existed as frontiers and barriers between countries. They have also encouraged the development of particular modes of transport.

Europe is surrounded by many seas: the Atlantic, North Sea, Baltic, Black Sea and the Mediterranean. The irregular coastline includes the peninsulas of Denmark, Scandinavia, Greece, Italy, and the Iberian Peninsula of Portugal and Spain. They are 'out on a limb' from the main landmass. When these countries, and the island of Britain, wanted to trade abroad they had to become seafaring nations.

The great central plain, which stretches from the Urals in the USSR westwards across to France's Atlantic coast, comprises two-thirds of the European landmass. Then there are the highland areas: the Alps, the Pyrenees, the mountains of Scandinavia, the Carpathians and the Urals. The mountains have tended to deter transport links, and have formed natural frontiers between countries.

Two great rivers, the Rhine and the Danube, flow north from the Alps. The Rhône and the Po flow south. In Eastern Europe the Rivers Volga, Don, Dnieper and Western Dvina flow from the Valdai Hills. These major river systems have provided natural lines of communication between northern and southern Europe. They remain important links for commerce and trade between countries.

The development of transport in Europe

Travellers, merchants and armies have always needed to move easily from one place to another, whether on water or on land. The Romans are famous for their roads which linked the corners of their huge empire. 'All roads lead to Rome', as the saying goes! They constructed more than 85,000 km of long, straight roads for military and trading purposes. Remarkably, the network of Roman roads remained the basis for European transport until the eighteenth century. At this time, an increase in trade led to a demand for improved transport links, which in turn led to a development of new road building techniques in France and Britain.

The new private or 'turnpike' roads, however, soon proved to be inadequate. Improved communication links were required during the economic expansion brought about by the industrial revolutions in Britain, France, Belgium and Germany. The more transport links were improved, the faster the new industrial cities grew, and so the need for more efficient transportation of people and goods also grew.

As a result, the nineteenth and twentieth centuries saw an astonishingly rapid advance in transport technology. Each new development led to a mode of transport faster than the one used before.

A painting by the nineteenth century artist, Turner, gives one impression of the early steam trains.

Canal transport was developed from the 1740s as a cheap but slow bulk carrier of products such as iron and cotton. Some canals were built around industrial areas, such as the Ruhr in Germany, providing links to the seaports. Other canals were built as short-cuts for shipping, such as the Kiel Canal linking the North Sea with the Baltic.

The first railway lines, built in Europe during the 1840s, were cheaper, faster, and able to carry larger quantities of freight than either coach and horse or the canals.

The importance of railways was not challenged until the increase in numbers of the private motor car

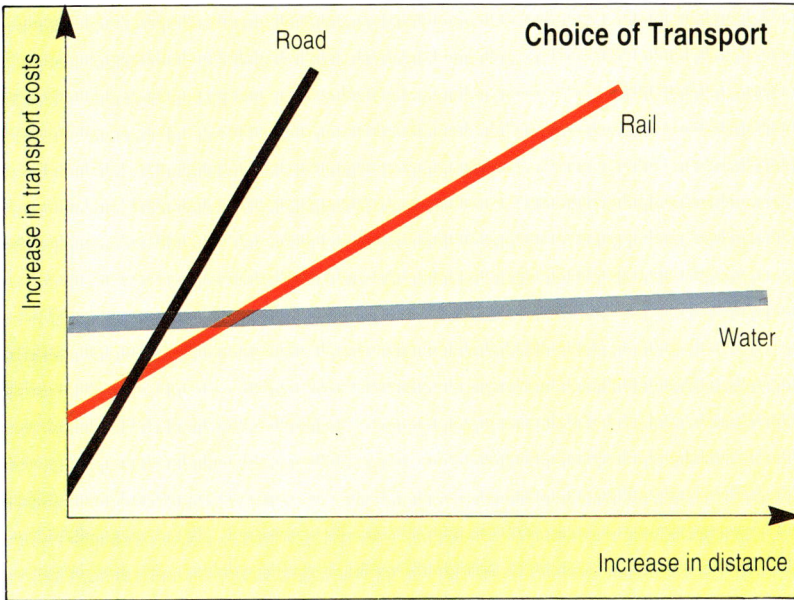

Choice of Transport

Road

Rail

Water

Increase in transport costs

Increase in distance

Above **A graph showing how the type of transport chosen will depend on the length of the journey.**

Left (top) **Designs for the so-called 'people's car' were around before the Second World War. It was not until peace was resumed, however, that mass-production of the German Volkswagon took place.**

Left (bottom) **A print of a nineteenth century London-Birmingham steam coach.**

in the 1920s. Motorways were first built in Germany during the 1930s by Hitler, who wanted a rapid transport system for his army. Since the 1960s a large network of motorways has been constructed throughout Europe.

The aircraft industry expanded rapidly in the late 1950s with the commercial development of the jet engine. It has become such an important mode of transport that 274 million passengers used air transport in the European Community (EC) in 1987.

THE DIFFERENT FORMS OF TRANSPORT

Different forms, or modes, of transport are suitable for different purposes. You would not choose to walk from John O'Groats to Athens – it's a huge distance, and it would

take too long! Flying would be a better idea if you have the money. Nor would you transport heavy goods such as coal by plane – it would cost too much. Taking the goods by ship, canal or train might be slower, but certainly cheaper.

Here are some of the points companies think about when deciding which mode of transport to use for moving goods:

● What kind of goods are they? Perishable items, like fresh fruit, have to be transported much more quickly than raw materials like coal or iron ore.

● How much will the transport cost?

● How long is the journey?

● What is the size and weight of the load?

The above graph shows how the cost of transporting freight by road, rail or canal increases with distance. It shows that road transport is the cheapest of all for short journeys, but is much more expensive for longer ones.

Rail is good value for medium-length journeys while, out of all the forms, canal transport is the cheapest of all for long journeys. In fact, the cost of canal transport does not increase much, regardless of the length of journey to be made.

Air travel is not included because it is so expensive for short journeys, and only gets cheaper for very long trips.

The chart below shows the percentage of freight that was transported by road, rail and inland water (canal or river) in each of the twelve member states of the EC in 1987. If no number is given, it means that nothing, or very little freight, was carried by that particular form of transport.

The chart can tell us a lot of useful information. Road is the main way of transporting freight in the EC. It is much more important in countries at the edge of the Community (UK, Ireland, Denmark, Greece, Spain and Portugal) than those at the centre. Why is this?

The answer lies with the importance of the River Rhine and other rivers which run into the North Sea. Germany, the Netherlands and Belgium carry large quantities of bulky freight by barge. They do not need to use road transport as much. It is also these three countries, along with France and Italy, which use their railways to transport freight much more than those at the edge of the Community.

The percentage of freight transported by road, rail and inland water (canal or river) by EC member states in 1987.

Country	Road	Rail	Inland Water
Germany	43	20	37
France	57	36	7
Italy	69	31	—
Netherlands	41	3	56
Belgium	57	16	27
Luxembourg	71	23	6
UK	97	3	—
Ireland	100	—	—
Denmark	94	6	—
Greece	100	—	—
Spain	92	8	—
Portugal	91	9	—

(A '—' means that nothing, or next to no freight is carried by that particular form of transport.)

Advantages of road transport

● It is convenient, and can go from door-to-door.

● It can get to places which other forms of transport cannot easily reach.

● It is the fastest and cheapest form of transportation over distances of less than 325 km.

● Other forms of transport still need road transport to take freight to railway stations, docks or airports before being moved by train, ship or plane.

Disadvantages

● It is slower and more expensive than railways over distances of more than 325 km.

● Traffic jams in cities make vehicles slow and inefficient.

● Road vehicles are responsible for polluting the environment far more than are trains or ships

● Road vehicles use up scarce

This Austrian motorway is typical of those found all over Europe.

resources like oil: half of the EC's total oil consumption is taken up by transport.

● Road accidents kill 44,000 people in the EC each year, and injure two million more.

Advantages of rail transport

● Rail is faster and cheaper than road for journeys of over 325 km.

● It uses fuel very efficiently, considering the large numbers of passengers that can be carried.

● It is a cheap way to transport freight in containers, or to move bulky items like coal.

● It is much safer than road transport.

● It is a more relaxing way to travel than by car.

Disadvantages

● Goods and people often have to rely on getting to and from railway stations by road transport. Trains can only travel where there are railway lines. This can be a problem when places are a long way from the nearest station.

● Trains run to fixed timetables, which are not always convenient.

● The cost of keeping the rail network in good running order is very high.

Advantages of air transport

● It is the fastest form of international travel.

● It is the safest way to travel.

Disadvantages

● Air transport is very expensive.

● It is not suited to bulky freight.

● Aeroplanes cause noise and pollution.

● Air transport is no good for short distances.

● A plane uses vast quantities of fuel – five times as much energy as a train to transport the same number of people.

Water transport

The advantage of inland water transport is that it can carry bulky freight for long distances at a low price. The main disadvantage is that, besides Belgium, the

A container is lowered on to a freight train. This method of transporting heavy goods over long distances is very efficient.

Bicycles are not only a means of personal transport, they are also a good form of entertainment.

Netherlands, France and Germany, no other EC countries have a network of waterways quite like the rivers Rhine or Rhône! Britain's canals, for example, which were very important during the Industrial Revolution, are today mainly used for pleasure craft.

Personal transport

Finally, what about walking and cycling? So far we have been looking at transport over long distances. Most travel is actually very local. Over one-third of all journeys are under 1.5 km in length, and 84 per cent of these are made on foot. More than half of all journeys are under 3 km.

For journeys of more than 4.5 km the use of the car or bus increases, and these are used most for journeys of between 16 and 40 km. For longer journeys, people tend to travel either by train or by car.

Children mainly walk to get anywhere. They are also driven around a lot, either by adults in cars, or on local buses. Teenagers tend to use bus, train and bicycle. Those who make most use of bikes in Britain are 11-15 year olds.

Transport policy for a united Europe

The first steps towards a combined European policy on transport were taken after the Second World War. The formation of the European Coal and Steel Community (ECSC) in 1951 sought to prevent further conflict in Europe by creating a common market for the production, sale and transport of the two most important industrial goods: coal and steel. Its founder members, known as 'The Six', were France, Germany, Italy, Luxembourg, the Netherlands and Belgium.

'The Six' formed the European Economic Community (EEC) in 1958. Its aims were to gradually unify the economies of its member states, and one day achieve political unity too. More than thirty years later the EC has gone a long way towards achieving its economic aims. From 'The Six' it has grown to twelve member states, and membership will probably continue to increase throughout the 1990s.

Above **Jacques Delors, President of the European Community. As the EC grows in political and economic power, policies on areas such as transport will become more uniform.**

Right **Amsterdam is renowned for its bicycles and trams.**

For a long time the EC did not really tackle the issue of transport. This is surprising, since good communication links are essential for the creation of an economic community. However, the issue has been a very complicated one. Each country has its own transport policies, and no two are the same. This is because the development of transport in a country depends on its geography, history, size, density of population and level of economic activity.

However, one can generalize and say that there have been two main forms of transport policy throughout Western Europe, the interventionist and the 'laissez-faire'.

Interventionist policy is when a government 'intervenes' in, or centrally plans, the development of transport, for example by financially aiding transport infrastructure. France, Germany and the Netherlands have followed this course much more than other countries because they have seen transport as a tool for achieving economic growth. The former Communist countries of Eastern Europe gave even more attention to the central planning of their transport networks.

'Laissez-faire' is French for 'let it be'. A 'laissez-faire' policy is when the government does not intervene in transport development, but just lets things happen in their own

way. Most 'laissez-faire' countries are at the periphery or edge of the EC, like Denmark, Ireland, Britain, Greece, Italy, Spain and Portugal. What these countries have in common is that they rely almost totally on road transport.

The development of a common EC transport policy has had to tiptoe through this political minefield. The problem has been how to link each country's own transport policy with a joint European one. It has not been easy.

1992: THE SINGLE EUROPEAN MARKET

There has been a lot of talk about the meaning of 1992, and the creation of the Single European Market (SEM). What is it all about, and what does it mean for transport?

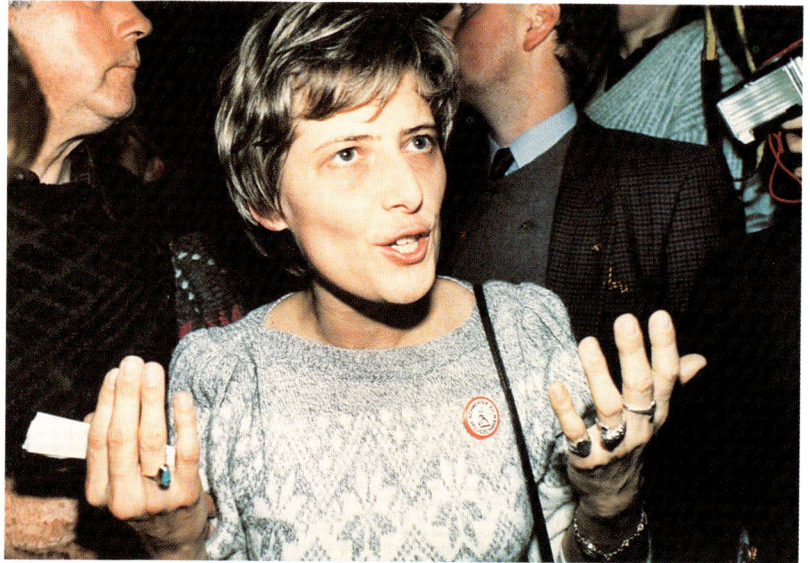

Petra Kelly is leader of Germany's green party. The issue of public transport is a priority for all of Europe's environmental groups.

1993 sees the twelve member states of the EC acting as a single economic unit or market. This involves the removal of internal barriers to trade, such as delays at frontiers, and the limits on the operation of lorries. Since 1985 over 300 separate laws have been passed to harmonize the separate trade regulations of the twelve EC members.

The SEM will have a huge effect on transport in the EC. Once in place, there will be complete freedom of movement of goods within the Community. This will particularly affect road haulage (goods carried by lorries), since it is the major way of transporting goods in the EC.

'Cabotage' is the name for a system which permits trucks from one EC country to freely pick up and transport goods to another. This new development may cut down the number of lorries returning home empty, although it may also lead to more lorries being on the road. Cabotage will probably increase competition between hauliers, bringing down the cost of road haulage and the price of goods in shops. However, it will also make rail freight a more expensive option, even though it is less damaging to the environment.

Should the EC continue to encourage lorry transport or should it give more support to transport by rail?

THE EUROPEAN HIGH-SPEED RAIL NETWORK

The growth of European cities in the nineteenth century relied upon railways to move people and goods from one place to another. In the days before cars and planes, trains ran with a speed and efficiency that had never been seen before.

By the 1950s, it was clear that railways were losing out to roads. Increasing numbers of people owned cars, and it was cheaper to

A map of the future European high-speed rail system.

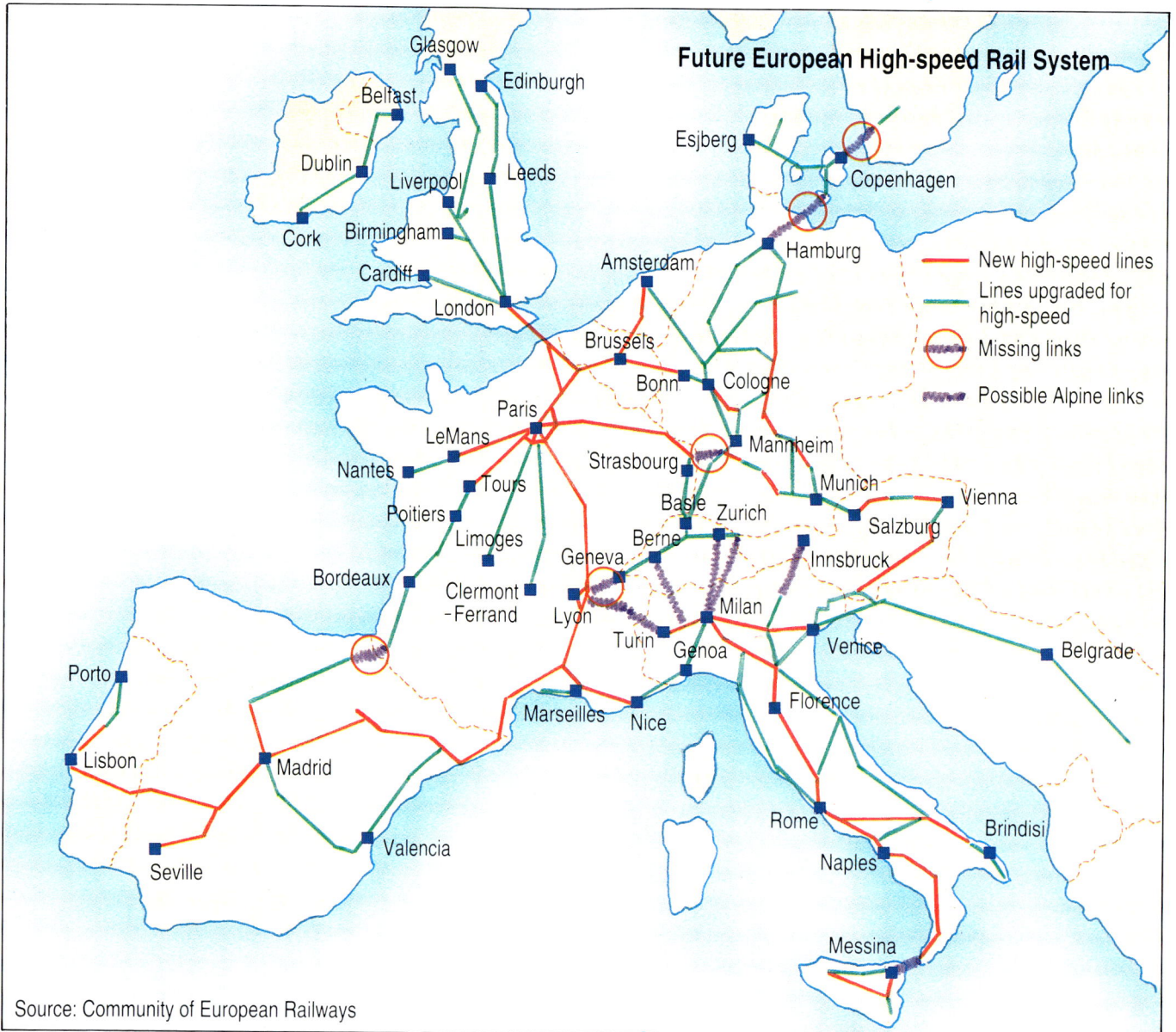

Future European High-speed Rail System

——	New high-speed lines
——	Lines upgraded for high-speed
⭕	Missing links
〰️	Possible Alpine links

Source: Community of European Railways

move freight short distances by road rather than by rail.

Yet there is talk that the 1990s will see the beginning of a new Rail Age. It is planned that by 2015 Europe's major cities will be linked by a high-speed rail network 15,000 km long. Its importance has been compared with the introduction of the jet engine in the 1950s, and the building of Europe's motorways in the 1960s.

At the heart of this network are France's new *Trains à Grande Vitesse* (TGVs, or high-speed trains). The first line, from Paris to Lyons, was opened in 1983. Its comfort, lower cost and speeds of up to 325 kph, convinced many business travellers to go by train rather than by plane.

The high speed train could replace air travel for journeys under 500 km. The Nord line, from Paris to the Channel Tunnel, has been built, and another to Belgium will link Paris and Brussels in 1993. By 2005 a major high-speed network of 4,400 km is planned in France alone.

The success of the TGV has encouraged Belgium, Germany and Italy to build their own high-speed rail networks. Spain is building a line from Barcelona to link up with the French network. The governments of these countries have made railways a priority in their transport planning. France and Germany both support their railways with four times more public money than Britain provides for British Rail.

The EC supports the idea of a European-wide network because it would take the pressure off congested air routes. Also, with increasing concern about the environment, the EC would like

fast trains to take freight transport off the roads and back onto the rails. This would reduce lorry traffic and pollution in the industrial Golden Triangle (see page 37), and the busy Trans-Alpine route between Germany and Italy. However, at the moment, trains carry only 10 per cent of Europe's freight.

THE CHANNEL TUNNEL

The Channel Tunnel plays an important part in the European transport system, linking London with Paris and Brussels.

The tunnel is seen in a very different light by the French, Belgian and British governments. The French want it to revive the stagnant economy of their depressed north-western region around Lille, bringing new jobs and services. They have invested in a new railway line from Calais to Paris, linking the tunnel with the European high-speed rail network. New links have also been built to connect it with the main airports at Paris and Brussels, and the cities' public transport systems.

The British government has refused to provide the tunnel with any public funding. All the money has come from private investors. The lack of high standard rail links beyond London has concerned companies in the Midlands, Wales, Scotland and Ireland that they will not benefit from the shorter time it will take to reach the European markets on the continent.

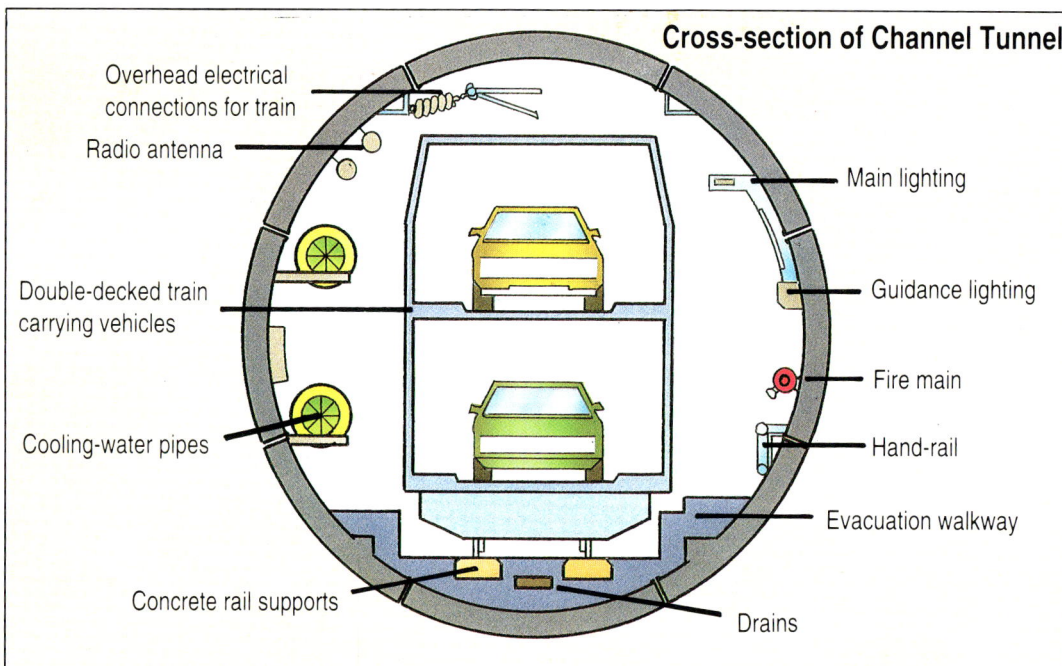

Cross-section of Channel Tunnel

Overhead electrical connections for train

Radio antenna

Double-decked train carrying vehicles

Cooling-water pipes

Concrete rail supports

Main lighting

Guidance lighting

Fire main

Hand-rail

Evacuation walkway

Drains

A cross-section of the Channel Tunnel showing the two-tiered train system, along with loaded cars.

Future European transport links

The construction of the Channel Tunnel is the single most expensive addition to Europe's transport system. However, there are many other less publicized links still required throughout the continent. Most European road and rail systems run along the valley floors of the major rivers, which generally flow along a north-south axis. There are far fewer running East-West. Already restricted for physical reasons, road and rail lines have been further limited by political factors.

This hydrofoil carries passengers to and from Moscow.

After the Second World War, Europe was split by an 'Iron Curtain' which separated the Communist East from the capitalist West. After the destruction caused by the War, East-West transport links were not replaced. Only now, in the aftermath of the cold war (see page 42), and with the end of Communism in Eastern Europe, are countries such as Poland, Hungary, Czechoslovakia and Romania once more looking westwards. A whole new, and very expensive, road and rail infrastructure will be required if a more unified Europe is to emerge.

Greece, Yugoslavia, Turkey and Albania

Greece is physically isolated from the other member states of the EC. Road and rail links have to first pass through Yugoslavia. A new 1000 km motorway, the Autoput, is being completed. Yugoslavia's only international road link, it will run from the Italian-Austrian border down to the Greek frontier. It will also improve the overland links with Turkey and the Middle East.

While under Communist dictatorship, Albania closed itself off from the rest of Europe. Its desire to change is indicated by the building of new rail links with Yugoslavia's network, and that of the world beyond.

Strait of Messina

The Italian government plans to build a bridge across the Strait of Messina that will link Sicily with Calabria, the region in the toe of the 'Italian boot'. Southern Italy, *the Mezzogiorno*, is much poorer and less developed than the industrial north. The idea is that improved transport links will aid economic development.

Scandinavia

Greece is not the only country which is a long distance from the important commercial markets of central mainland Europe. So are the Scandinavian countries of Norway, Sweden and Finland.

The Great Belt Fixed Link between Sweden, Copenhagen's island of Sjaeland, and Jutland will open in the mid-1990s. It will comprise a combination of road bridges and rail tunnels.

New passes through the Alps and the Pyrenees

The Alps and the Pyrenees have long been a physical barrier to inter-European communication. Passes built in the nineteenth century through the Alps, the Simplon, Gothard and Brenner routes, are no longer sufficient to carry the increasing quantity of trade between Italy, Austria and Germany.

The Trans-Alpine bottleneck, as it has been called, has led to friction between Austria and Italy. Austria objects to the noise, road damage and pollution caused by huge Italian juggernaut lorries. It prefers container traffic to be carried by rail (see pages 35-7 on combined transport). Rail tunnels are to be widened to allow for double lines of tracks.

Left **Many parts of Eastern Europe, poor by Western standards, have problems in obtaining fuel for transport.**

Right **Future transport links across Europe.**

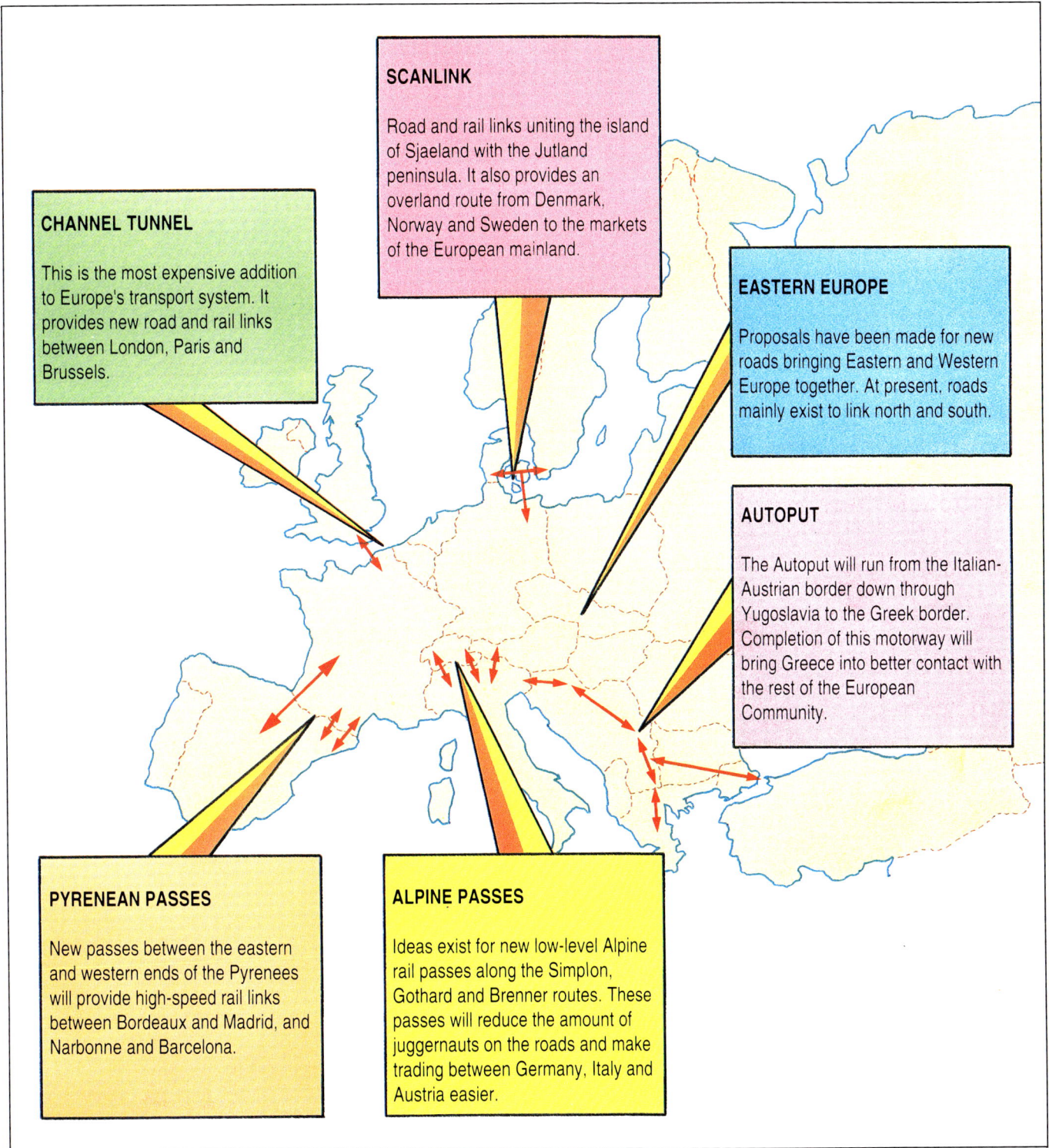

SCANLINK

Road and rail links uniting the island of Sjaeland with the Jutland peninsula. It also provides an overland route from Denmark, Norway and Sweden to the markets of the European mainland.

CHANNEL TUNNEL

This is the most expensive addition to Europe's transport system. It provides new road and rail links between London, Paris and Brussels.

EASTERN EUROPE

Proposals have been made for new roads bringing Eastern and Western Europe together. At present, roads mainly exist to link north and south.

AUTOPUT

The Autoput will run from the Italian-Austrian border down through Yugoslavia to the Greek border. Completion of this motorway will bring Greece into better contact with the rest of the European Community.

PYRENEAN PASSES

New passes between the eastern and western ends of the Pyrenees will provide high-speed rail links between Bordeaux and Madrid, and Narbonne and Barcelona.

ALPINE PASSES

Ideas exist for new low-level Alpine rail passes along the Simplon, Gothard and Brenner routes. These passes will reduce the amount of juggernauts on the roads and make trading between Germany, Italy and Austria easier.

Transport in Eastern Europe

Fewer people own a car in Eastern Europe and the USSR than in Western Europe. However, car ownership there has increased by more than five times in twenty years, from 6 million in 1970 to 34 million in 1988. Since the end of Communist rule in 1989, car ownership has again increased rapidly. As a response to the previous lack of consumer goods, the car has come to symbolize personal freedom for many Eastern Europeans.

Volkswagen have bought Czechoslovakia's car manufacturers, Skoda, in the hope of expanding the market there. The motorway network in Eastern European countries is very limited. Poland has only 100 km of motorway.

The priority for the Communist governments was to provide a good public transport service, and this they did. The metros in Moscow and Leningrad are famous as works of art. Of the 300 tram systems in the world, 110 are in the USSR, with 70 more in Eastern Europe. Taxis are popular in cities: there are 20,000 of them in Budapest, the capital of Hungary, compared to just 4,000 in Vienna in Austria.

Railways are often only single-tracked, and journeys are slow but cheap. Belgrade and Sofia, the capitals of Yugoslavia and Bulgaria, are about 320 km apart. There are only two trains per day, and the journey takes ten hours. This is the same distance as between Preston and London; these latter two places are connected by hourly trains, with a journey time of only three hours.

New rail passes are proposed at the eastern and western ends of the Pyrenees. They will ease the way for the new high-speed rail links between Bordeaux and Madrid on the western side, and Narbonne and Barcelona on the eastern side. A new central road pass is also planned.

Strait of Gibraltar

There are plans to build a tunnel or bridge between Spain and Morocco. For Morocco, this would be a very prestigious project, symbolically linking North Africa with Europe.

Left **Moscow's underground system is famed for its beautiful architecture.**

Road transport

The convenience of driving from door-to-door led to a decline in the amount of freight carried by rail in the 1950s. Today 85 per cent of EC freight is carried by road. The food and construction industries rely heavily on road transport. In the 1960s motorways were built to keep traffic moving. Some are truly European motorways, passing from one end of the continent to the other. For example, the E75 goes all the way from the Polish port of Gdansk to Thessaloniki in Greece.

An increase in the maximum weight for heavy goods vehicles (HGVs) from 32.5 to 38 tonnes has meant more trade without a

Europe's busiest roads.

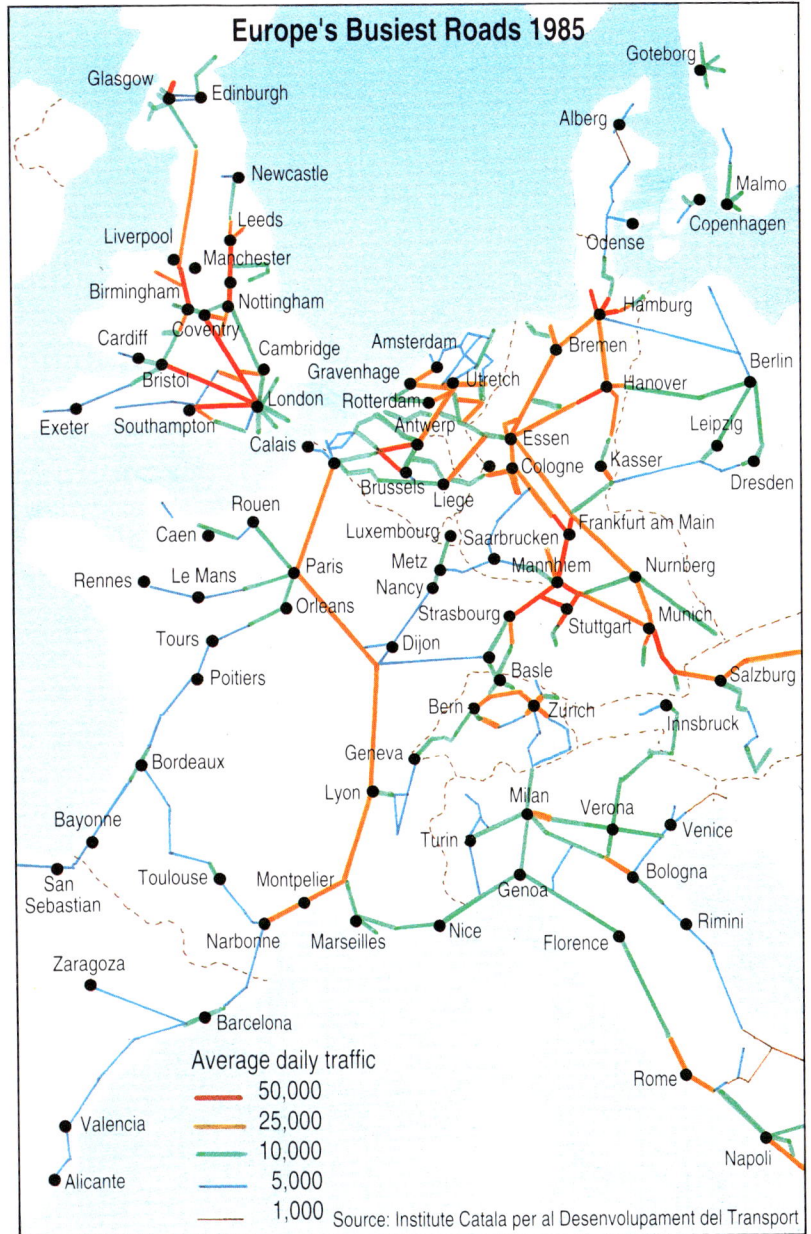

Europe's Busiest Roads 1985

Glasgow • Edinburgh • Newcastle • Leeds • Liverpool • Manchester • Birmingham • Nottingham • Cardiff • Coventry • Bristol • Cambridge • London • Exeter • Southampton • Calais

Goteborg • Alberg • Malmo • Copenhagen • Odense • Hamburg • Bremen • Berlin • Hanover • Leipzig • Essen • Kasser • Cologne • Dresden

Amsterdam • Gravenhage • Utretch • Rotterdam • Antwerp • Brussels • Liege • Rouen • Caen • Rennes • Le Mans • Paris • Orleans • Tours • Poitiers • Luxembourg • Saarbrucken • Metz • Nancy • Mannhem • Strasbourg • Dijon • Frankfurt am Main • Nurnberg • Munich • Stuttgart • Salzburg • Basle • Bern • Zurich • Innsbruck • Bordeaux • Bayonne • Geneva • Lyon • Milan • Verona • Venice • Turin • Bologna • Genoa • Rimini • San Sebastian • Toulouse • Montpelier • Nice • Florence • Narbonne • Marseilles • Zaragoza • Barcelona • Rome • Valencia • Napoli • Alicante

Average daily traffic

50,000	
25,000	
10,000	
5,000	
1,000	

Source: Institute Catala per al Desenvolupament del Transport

corresponding increase in traffic.

The chart below shows (1) the number of vehicles per kilometre of motorway and (2) the length of motorways in four EC countries.

Country	1	2
France	34	6570
Netherlands	50	2060
UK	60	2992
West Germany	62	8715
		1988 figures

The Netherlands, one-sixth the size of Britain, has two-thirds the kilometres of motorway. Before unification with East Germany, West Germany was not much bigger than Britain but had three times the length of motorways.

Road safety

The chart on the right shows (1) the density of population per square kilometre, (2) the number of cars and taxis per thousand people, and (3) road deaths per million people (1988 figures).

What can we learn from the chart? You might think that a country with low population density and a relatively small number of cars per thousand people would have fewer road deaths than more populated countries. But this is not the case,

particularly if you compare the Netherlands with Portugal.

CARS AND CITIES

Cars and cities do not mix. That has been the decision which most European large cities and capitals

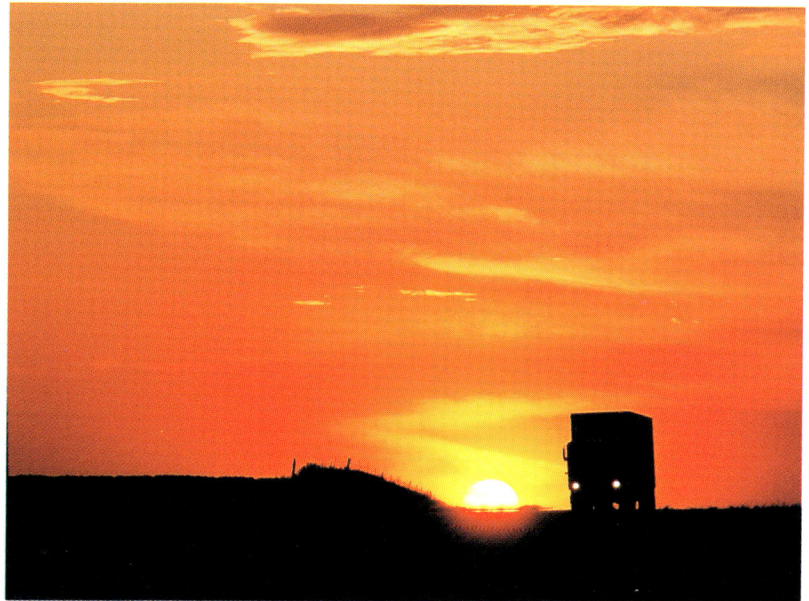

As the sun starts to go down, this lorry sets off on its long-distance journey from one European country to another.

Country	1	2	3
West Germany	246	473	309
Spain	77	296	612
France	101	451	482
UK	236	364	272
Italy	190	425	311
Netherlands	352	371	282
Portugal	108	246	1071
Sweden	17	417	241
			1988 figures

Right **The cars we use everyday are eventually discarded, adding to the already huge problem of refuse disposal in Europe.**

have arrived at in the early 1990s. Until the 1960s the car was king. Town planners thought first in terms of roads, and then in terms of people. This led to plans being drawn up for building multi-level motorways through central London in the 1950s. Although the plans were dropped because of public opposition, they demonstrated the high priority that cars were given.

Some would say that cars are killing European cities. In 1985 Athens took an extreme measure to combat congestion within the city, and the pollution of its ancient monuments, caused by cars. It permitted car owners to bring their vehicles into the city centre only on alternate days. What happened? Many Athenians went out and bought a second car. Instead of decreasing traffic, 70,000 more cars appeared on the roads.

Cities throughout Europe are still experimenting with different techniques for dealing with the need to transport large numbers of people and goods efficiently. But can this be balanced with the need to make cities more pleasant places for the residents to live in?

As you will read in the following pages, many countries have decided to improve their public transport systems, and make car driving more expensive, in order to reduce the congestion in their cities. Traffic jams cost a country's economy millions of pounds in wasted time.

Road pricing

Norway's capital, Oslo, has introduced a road-pricing scheme where drivers automatically pay every time they take the car through the city. There are plans to charge higher fees at peak times, so as to discourage non-essential journeys.

Below **A traffic jam by the Arc de Triumphe, Paris.**

Greenpeace action at a motorshow in Brussels, Belgium.

The scheme works by using electronic toll gates around the city. Every time a car passes one, a signal is sent out, bounces off a small electronic block attached to the car, and identifies the driver who is then billed accordingly.

In this way motorists are paying for a road improvement scheme which has included the building of a road tunnel underneath the city. The tunnel has halved the time it takes to cross Oslo. Sweden's capital, Stockholm, also had plans to introduce an electronic road toll system as a way in which road users would pay for road improvements. However, public opposition has meant that the city will not be going ahead with its road-pricing scheme.

'Red routes'

Both Paris and London are famous for their traffic problems. For example, in Paris more than one and a half million vehicles drive around the city every day, at an average speed of 13 kph. There is only one parking place for every two cars. Paris has three times as many traffic jams as in the whole of the rest of France.

In London, two million vehicles drive around the city every day. Average traffic speed is 20 kph, 3 kph slower than 50 years ago. Bicycles travel faster! Yet, for all of the congestion caused by road traffic, it is only 14 per cent of people who travel by car in London. Almost 80 per cent of people travel by public transport: 40 per cent by train, and nearly as many again by bus and underground.

In both cities the authorities hoped drivers would see how bad the problem was, and make their own decision to start using public transport instead. This did not happen. So, in an attempt to keep traffic moving, certain key roads have been called 'red routes' and vehicles are prevented from parking or waiting on these roads. While traffic has begun to move faster, shopkeepers have complained of losing customers.

The 'green' tax

Critics of cars and lorries argue that owners should pay large 'hidden costs' that result from road use. Hidden costs include the full expense of road-building, accidents and pollution, which are paid for by government, or not at all.

The idea behind the scheme is that when people pay the full costs of driving, they might then use their cars less often, and public transport more often.

In Britain, cars and lorries pay only about 25 per cent of the hidden costs to the government in the form of an annual road tax, and a tax on fuel. A 'green' tax would increase the tax on fuel, so as to pay for the cars' true costs. This idea, known as ecological taxation reform, has been developed in Germany.

'Woonerven': living yards

Woonerf is a Dutch word meaning 'living yard'. It is an area specially designed in the residential part of a city where children, pedestrians, cyclists and cars can all mix safely and freely.

Roads are redesigned, and much traffic re-routed onto main roads. The needs of local people are put first. Introduced in the Netherlands in the mid-1970s, vehicle speeds are reduced to walking speed in these special areas. Car drivers are held responsible for accidents that involve children. A road sign at the entrance to *woonerven* reminds drivers of their need to slow right down. The idea can be found in many northern European cities, especially in the Netherlands and Germany.

'Verkehrsberuhigung': traffic-calming measures

Translated literally from the German, *verkehrsberuhigung* means traffic-calming. During the

economic recession of the 1980s in Western Europe, the cost of building *woonerven* became too expensive. Traffic-calming has proved to be a cheaper method of forcing cars to reduce speed.

Residential roads are narrowed, road humps are laid, and trees and flowers planted in the street. Not only do cars then have to drive more slowly, but the streets become more pleasant for the residents.

There are thousands of examples of traffic-calming throughout Germany. It has made such a difference in the town of Freiburg that 25 per cent of journeys there are now made by bicycle!

The idea has proved very popular in Sweden, Italy, Switzerland and Denmark. Dutch cities like Delft, Groningen and Maastricht have introduced traffic-calming measures to more than 30 per cent of their residential areas.

Right **Less traffic on the roads, as a result of Swedish traffic-calming measures, has made life easier for this taxi driver.**

29

Many shopping areas throughout Europe have been pedestrianized.

PEDESTRIANS AND PEDESTRIANIZATION

When you think about transport, cars are among the first things that come to mind. Certainly, road transport is very important in Europe. But so is walking. If transport is about the movement of people and goods from one place to another, then what are you doing when walking home with something from the shops?

In fact, one-third of all travel time is spent walking, and more than one-third of all journeys are made on foot. Very few transport statistics take this into account when they show the relative importance of cars, trains, planes and ships. This is because transport statistics ignore journeys of less than 1.5 km. However, 84 per cent of these short journeys are undertaken on foot!

Those who rely on their feet as a mode of transport also tend to be those who rely on public transport: the young, mothers with children, and the elderly.

On the continent, countries like the Netherlands and Germany take pedestrians seriously. Cars have been banned from many city centres, and main shopping areas have been pedestrianized. Munich has created a pedestrian zone of 85,000 square metres. Shoppers leave their cars at home, and use the excellent public transport services. Shopkeepers feared pedestrianization would mean less business, but in fact after one year, sales had increased by more than 25 per cent.

Public transport

Public transport is the main form of travel in cities, and is essential to those who have no other means of getting about. It offers a way of carrying large numbers of people rapidly, safely, and cheaply to their destinations.

Public transport generally includes buses or trains, but there are many different forms. Buses range from minibuses to double-length vehicles. There are four main types of rail service:

● Rapid rail operates in tunnels or on elevated tracks. Examples are the London or Moscow Underground, the Paris Metro and the German U-Bahn.

● Trams (or streetcars) are buses that run on rails, powered by overhead electric wires. They operate in city streets, alongside road traffic. They are common in Eastern European cities such as Prague. Britain got rid of most of its trams after the Second World War. Cities such as Manchester however, have recently reintroduced them.

● Light rail is a more modern version of the tram, but quieter and faster. It can run on its own track (like the Docklands Light Railway in London) or, like trams, alongside other road traffic. Germany has developed the use of this system a lot since the 1970s.

● Suburban or regional trains are designed to connect cities with their surrounding areas. The Paris RER is a very impressive high-speed rail system which runs underground through the city centre, and above ground outside it.

Left **People waiting to board a Spanish bus.**

Coventry

The British city of Coventry was virtually destroyed during the Second World War. During the 1950s the city planners rebuilt the city with the idea that very soon every family would own a car. A new road system was built.

The new city was constructed with different zones, each serving a different purpose. Housing was in one zone, shopping in another, and the factories in yet another. The idea was for people to use their cars to get from one zone to another.

However, by the 1970s and 1980s a very different picture had emerged. The 60 per cent of people with access to a car made use of the new shopping centres and multiplex cinemas built on the city's edge. Inner-city shops could not compete with the lower prices of the large shopping centres, and many went out of business. To many, the city centre had become a faceless place. The 40 per cent of inhabitants without access to a car – the less wealthy, the young and the elderly – relied on an inadequate public transport bus system.

Public pressure has led the city council to consider building an integrated public transport system like the German city of Hanover's, including a tram-way and cycle lanes.

Transport can be used for entertainment as well as a way of getting from one place to another. Here, this crowd is gathering for a pleasure-boat trip.

Hanover

The city of Hanover in northern Germany is twinned with Coventry. It, too, was largely destroyed by bombing during the Second World War. However, Hanover's city planners rebuilt the city along very different lines to those of Coventry. They decided to discourage car use, and instead build a good public transport system.

Unlike Coventry, Hanover rebuilt its pre-war tram system. The tram network did not have to be as large as it would be in Coventry because of Germany's different style of city housing. People live in blocks of apartments rather than their own semi-detached houses. This means that the city is more compact than Coventry, with a higher density of people living in a smaller area.

Cars were banned from the city centre, which was then pedestrianized. The efficient public transport service encourages people to leave their cars at home, and travel into town by tram, or by light rail which travels underground. The use of traffic-calming measures (see page 29) encourages people to use their bicycles much more.

Hanover's system of transport, which is capable of moving large numbers of people around by different modes of transport, is called an integrated rapid urban transit system.

The number of cars on European roads increases by 5 per cent every year. Here, cars pull in at a drive-in McDonald's in Birmingham.

The advantages of public transport are that it offers mobility for all but reduces congestion on the roads (the passengers from one London bus would fill 22 cars). It also cuts down on fuel consumption, and reduces pollution. To be successful, public transport has to be reliable. People get very frustrated if they have to wait too long for a bus or train.

Countries such as Germany, France and the Netherlands have improved their public transport systems in order to combat the congestion and pollution caused by cars. Unfortunately, Britain cut back its financial support for public transport during the 1980s.

Above **This tram is used everyday by thousands of Viennese commuters.**

In Europe, 70 per cent of the population is urban-dwelling. Many of the people commute, repeating the same journey between work, school and home every weekday morning and evening. This daily pattern leads to peak periods, or rush hours. Public transport has been designed to cope with these peaks. Urban commuters often use a combination of different forms of public transport for their journeys.

Right **The golden 'M' of the Paris Metro.**

Combined transport

Road, rail, air and shipping are the main ways, or modes, of transporting goods in Europe. Often a journey will involve using more than just one mode of transport. For example, imported products might be shipped to a port from where they are distributed by rail, then by road.

Containers are loaded on to ships at Rotterdam, Europe's largest port.

Combined transport is a new development. This is when freight is easily transferred from one mode of transport to another. Crucial to this new development has been the introduction of the container.

Containerized freight

The container is a steel box. It is loaded with freight by the sender, and can easily be transferred between container ships, rail, lorry or barge *en route* to its destination.

The introduction of container transport has dramatically changed the handling of freight, and nowhere more so than at sea ports. Forty years ago, merchandise used to be unloaded at the dockside by stevedores and dockers using cranes and nets.

The advent of the container led

to widespread unemployment among dockers, since huge straddle cranes could do the work of many people. Rotterdam, Harwich and Marseilles were quick to adapt their port facilities to deal with containers.

Combined road and rail traffic is called piggy-back transport. Containers are loaded onto trains from lorries, and taken 'piggy-back' to the rail depot closest to their final destination, where they are picked up and delivered by lorry. *Intercontainer* is an enterprise owned by twenty-five European rail companies for the international carriage of containers. Average journey length is 925 km, and most long-distance traffic is carried at night.

ROAD-RAIL TRANSPORT

Road-rail transport has sometimes been called a 'rolling motorway'. There are now more than 4,000 piggy-back consignments per day in Europe. This is equivalent to a daily line of lorries 70 km long being transferred from road to rail. Germany and France were the first to develop the system, and Italy is increasing its use of it.

Piggy-back transport has a lot to recommend it. Because of the heavy pressure of traffic on the few roads which pass through the Alps, it is well supported by the Alpine countries of France, Germany, Italy, Switzerland and Austria. It has proved to be less environmentally destructive, more reliable and safer to carry containers by rail.

From water to land: this lorry has collected its container from a port and now carries the goods by motorway across the country.

COMBINED WATER TRANSPORT

Inland waterways provide the necessary infrastructure for dealing with containers. The Rhine has improved its road and rail connections for 30 new container terminals between Emmerich and Basel. New barges, 10 m wide, can carry four containers across the width of the vessel. Co-ordinating the movements of container barges on the Rhine with the arrival and departure of seagoing vessels at Rotterdam's Superpoort has increased the system's competitiveness with road transport. Between 1977 and 1988 the number of containers transported on inland waterways in the EC increased 70 times.

'Ro-Ro' vessels can carry lorries and other vehicles. The term is short for 'roll on, roll off' because the cars and lorries drive on at one end of the ship, and drive off at the other. This makes them very quick to load and offload.

Along with car transporter barges, Ro-Ro vessels are a new innovation on the inland waterways of the Rhine. Loading platforms have been built for them at Mainz and Mannheim in Germany.

Many cross-channel ferries are of the 'Ro-Ro' sort. Serious questions about their safety and design were asked at a public enquiry when the *Herald of Free*

Transport in the Netherlands

The Netherlands is one of the smallest countries in Europe, yet when it comes to transport, it is one of the most important.

It handles 52 per cent of all the inland waterway freight in the EC, and 17 per cent of all road haulage, which is as much as France and Germany, countries several times larger than itself. Overall, it handles 25 per cent of all trade that goes on between the twelve member states of the EC.

There are several reasons for this. The Netherlands is at the heart of Europe's industrial backbone, the Golden Triangle. The region stretches north-south between Glasgow in Scotland, Frankfurt in Germany, and Milan in Italy. In relation to its size, the Golden Triangle contains the largest concentration of people (70 million), wealth and industry in the world.

In a sense the Netherlands is the front door to the Golden Triangle, and the river Rhine its main corridor. International shipping offloads at Rotterdam's Superpoort on the North Sea, and freight is then transported inland by barge up the Rhine to Germany, France, Switzerland and beyond. In 1987 more than two million containers either entered or left Rotterdam by sea.

Enterprise, a large roll on, roll off ferry, capsized off Zeebrugge, Belgium, in 1987, with the loss of many lives.

Water transport

Britain, Belgium, the Netherlands, France and Germany had huge shipping fleets in the nineteenth century, when they still had colonies in the developing world. Raw materials such as cotton were imported from the colonies, and finished products such as cloth were exported back to them. Sea transport is still vital for Europe's foreign trade with the rest of the world. However, in the 1970s and 1980s European shipping fleets suffered from an economic recession. For example, an increase in oil prices meant that less crude oil was imported by oil tanker from Saudi Arabia.

The decrease in trade led to the EC's commercial shipping fleet decreasing in size. In 1980 it accounted for 30 per cent of world shipping, but only 20 per cent in 1987. Greece had a fleet of 40,000 gross registered tonnes (grt) in 1980 which fell to 27,000 grt by 1986. Britain has suffered particularly badly in the slump, having lost three-fifths of its fleet between 1980 and 1986.

European shipping has also lost out to competition from cheaper south-east Asian fleets. Other shipping companies use 'flags of convenience', like those of Liberia or Panama, in order to avoid having to pay various taxes.

Piraeus, near Athens, is the main centre for the Greek shipping industry.

Coal being transported by barge down the River Rhine.

Despite the downturn in shipping, Rotterdam's Superpoort remains the most important port in the world: 43 per cent of all shipments from the United States to Europe, and 34 per cent of all shipments from Japan to Western Europe enter through Rotterdam. Many international companies use the port as the base from which to distribute their goods around Europe. Harwich in Britain and Marseilles in France are also large ports.

Large and speedy cellular container ships are often used on transatlantic crossings. They can carry as many as 2,000 six metre containers. They are called cellular because the ship is divided into units or cells, which make loading easier.

The majority of large commercial ships are known as bulk carriers. Wet bulk carriers transport crude oil from Saudi Arabia to the European refineries. Dry bulk carriers transport anything from coal to grain to iron ore. Ship sizes vary between those of the huge bulk carriers and the smaller barges which carry freight up and down the inland waterways of the rivers Rhine and Danube.

A new link joining the Rhine and Danube opening in the early 1990s will mean that freight offloaded at Rotterdam can be carried right through the waterways of West and East Europe as far as the Black Sea.

FERRY SERVICES

Passenger ships range from ocean-going liners to cross-channel ferries and hovercrafts. Some argue that the Channel Tunnel will bring about an end to cross-channel ferry services, but the ferry companies themselves disagree. They are upgrading the quality of their ships and hoping to keep in business. Ferries are also used between Greece and Italy, North Africa and Marseilles, Britain and Scandinavia, and between East and West across the Baltic Sea.

Air transport

It is a symbol of national pride for each European country to have its own airline. British Airways, Air France and Germany's Lufthansa are all household names. The map on page 43 shows the major European air routes, airports, and the number of passengers carried by West European airlines in 1988. Traditionally, each airline has flown to all major European capitals. At the same time it has limited the number of flights to its own country by other companies, to help prevent competition.

This has led to busy skies and artificially high prices on very short routes. The structure and organization of air transport in Europe will change dramatically throughout the 1990s.

Air Portugal is just one of the many European airlines in business today.

AIRLINE DEREGULATION

The rules and regulations that have protected national airlines from foreign competition will be removed. This is called 'deregulation'. The EC argues that increased competition will lead to lower fares and a greater choice of routes for travellers.

However, one should look at what deregulation has meant in other countries. In the United States, airlines were deregulated in 1978. Since then over 200

American airlines have gone out of business or been taken over by other companies.

It is likely that the same will happen in Europe. The big, successful companies are likely to get bigger. The smaller ones may not be able to compete, and may go bankrupt. The effect of the Gulf War in 1991 led to cut-backs by many European airlines, both big and small.

In order to protect themselves from possible take-over, many of the smaller airlines are clubbing together. Austrian Airlines, Swissair, Finair (Finland), and SAS (Sweden, Denmark and Norway) have agreed to jointly share major costs such as buying new planes, and still offer the important intercontinental routes.

The Anglo-French Concorde first flew in 1969, and remains the world's only successful supersonic airliner.

THE TRANSPORT HUB

British Airways carries more passengers per year than any other airline in the world. However, it is unlikely that London's Gatwick airport will remain Europe's most important transport hub. If you think of a wheel, with the hub at the centre, and the spokes fanning out, the airport is the hub, and its road and rail links are the spokes.

Gatwick has fewer 'spokes' than either Charles de Gaulle airport at Paris, or Brussels airport. What France and Belgium have done is to link these airports with the new high-speed rail network. By 2005, international travellers will be able to fly into these airports, and then take the high-speed train from them to most major European cities.

Security is vital at airports. These passengers are waiting to have their baggage checked on to the plane before they themselves board.

EUROPEAN AIR TRAFFIC CONTROL

The sky above us is vast and looks so empty. Yet the skies over Europe, particularly those over the Golden Triangle, are the busiest in the world. Air traffic control (ATC) is the system used to guide aircraft, and keep them a safe distance apart from each other.

Eurocontrol is the name for the European air traffic control system which was launched in 1965. It was meant to co-ordinate the flight paths of aircraft over Europe, but it was not a success. More than 25 years later, its time has come.

There are 42 different air traffic control centres, operating 22 different computer control systems in Europe. This is simply too dangerous. Danger is increased by the fact that many flights within Europe are short ones, less than 475 km. Much of the flight-time is spent ascending and descending. If airports are crowded, as many

of them are, this is the time when accidents are most likely to happen.

During descent, aircraft are 'stacked', one on top of another, and they land in strict rotation. London's Heathrow airport is so busy that one plane lands every minute. Such pressure puts a lot of strain on the present air traffic control system. That pressure will continue to increase. Many estimates say that European air traffic density will double by the year 2005. Already, the higher altitude air space is full to capacity.

The end of the cold war (the situation where a state of hostility and mistrust existed between the USSR and the Western world) is good news for air traffic controllers. Aircraft fly along particular lanes or 'corridors', depending on whether they are military or civil planes. Now that the USSR is seen as less of a military threat to the West, it is possible that more military air corridors will be opened up to civilian aircraft. This would relieve some of the congestion.

What Eurocontrol offers is a single ATC system for the whole continent, based in Brussels. Like the SEM, Eurocontrol aims to overcome national boundaries so as to make one large unit, rather than many little ones.

One strength of Eurocontrol is that it will include Eastern European ATCs. It will be linked with Moscow and Czechoslovakia. Since many East European countries have not modernized their own systems for many years, they can switch to Eurocontrol's high-technology system more easily than many West European countries. However, this will be very expensive for them, and the question remains: who will pay the bill?

The most frequently used air routes across Europe.

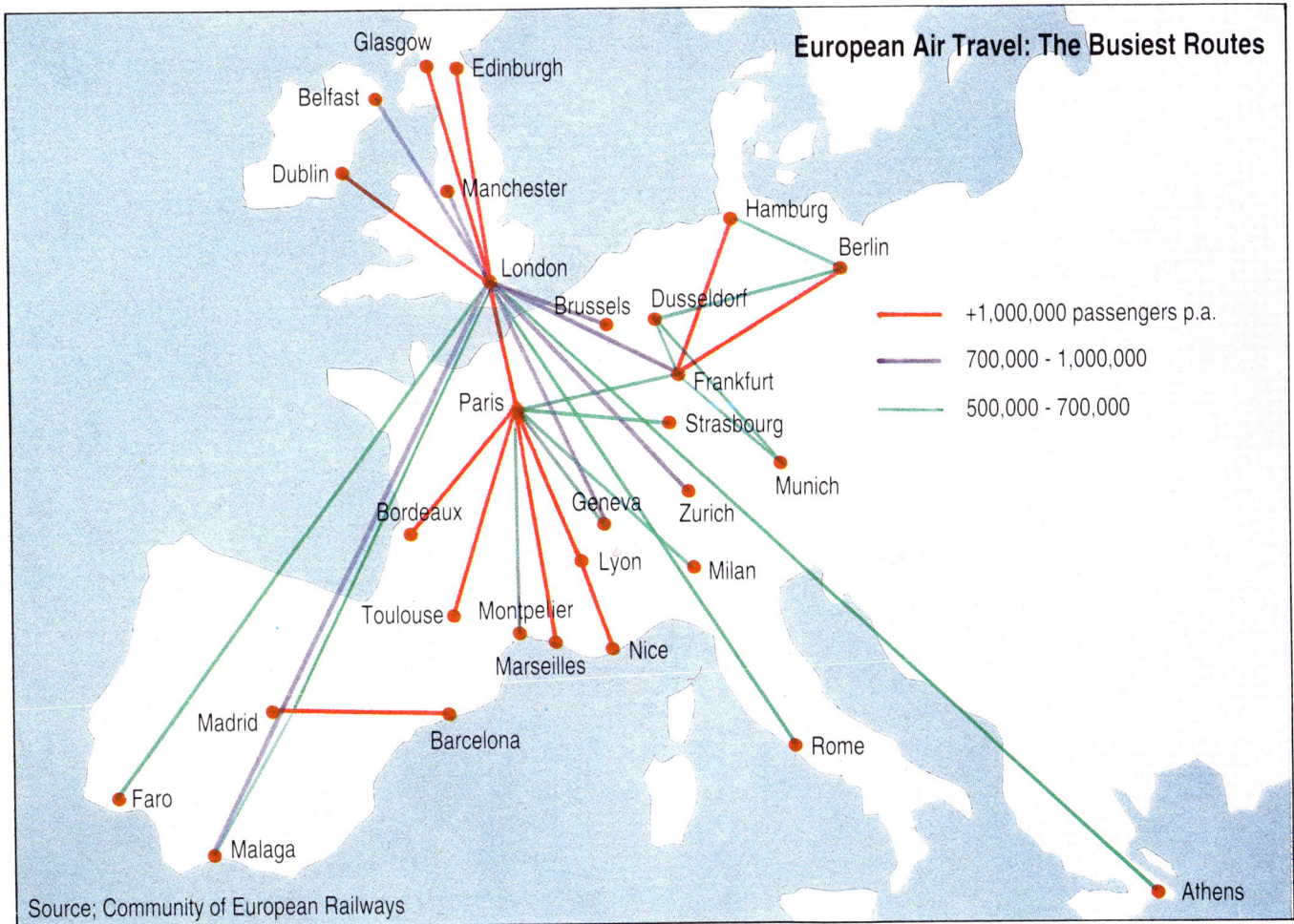

European Air Travel: The Busiest Routes

+1,000,000 passengers p.a.
700,000 - 1,000,000
500,000 - 700,000

Source; Community of European Railways

The way ahead

Improved transport links between different parts of the continent are bringing European countries ever closer together and speeding up travel times. Not since the last Ice Age, ten thousand years ago, has Britain been joined to the continent. With the Channel Tunnel, London is only three hours away from Brussels or Paris. This is good news for passengers and for business. The extension of the high-speed rail network beyond France will link the main cities in the Golden Triangle. Its speed will challenge the airlines which presently operate within Europe. The smaller airlines already face a less secure future, with increasing competition from the larger operators.

For some countries the answer to road congestion in cities has been to improve public transport services. The issue of road safety has led to strict controls on cars in residential areas in Germany and the Netherlands. Awareness about environmental pollution caused by road vehicles has persuaded some countries such as Austria to increase the amount of freight they send by rail.

The number of vehicles on the EC's already overcrowded roads is increasing by 5 per cent each year. Many argue that building more roads is not the answer, since they only attract more traffic and congestion.

Of all Europe's transport issues faced in the 1990s, the question of road transport will probably be the most difficult to solve.

Above **Good public transport will have to become high on the list of Europe's goals.**

Left **Unleaded petrol on sale in France: car users today are starting to think about the environment their children will grow up in.**

Right **The formation of the EC.**

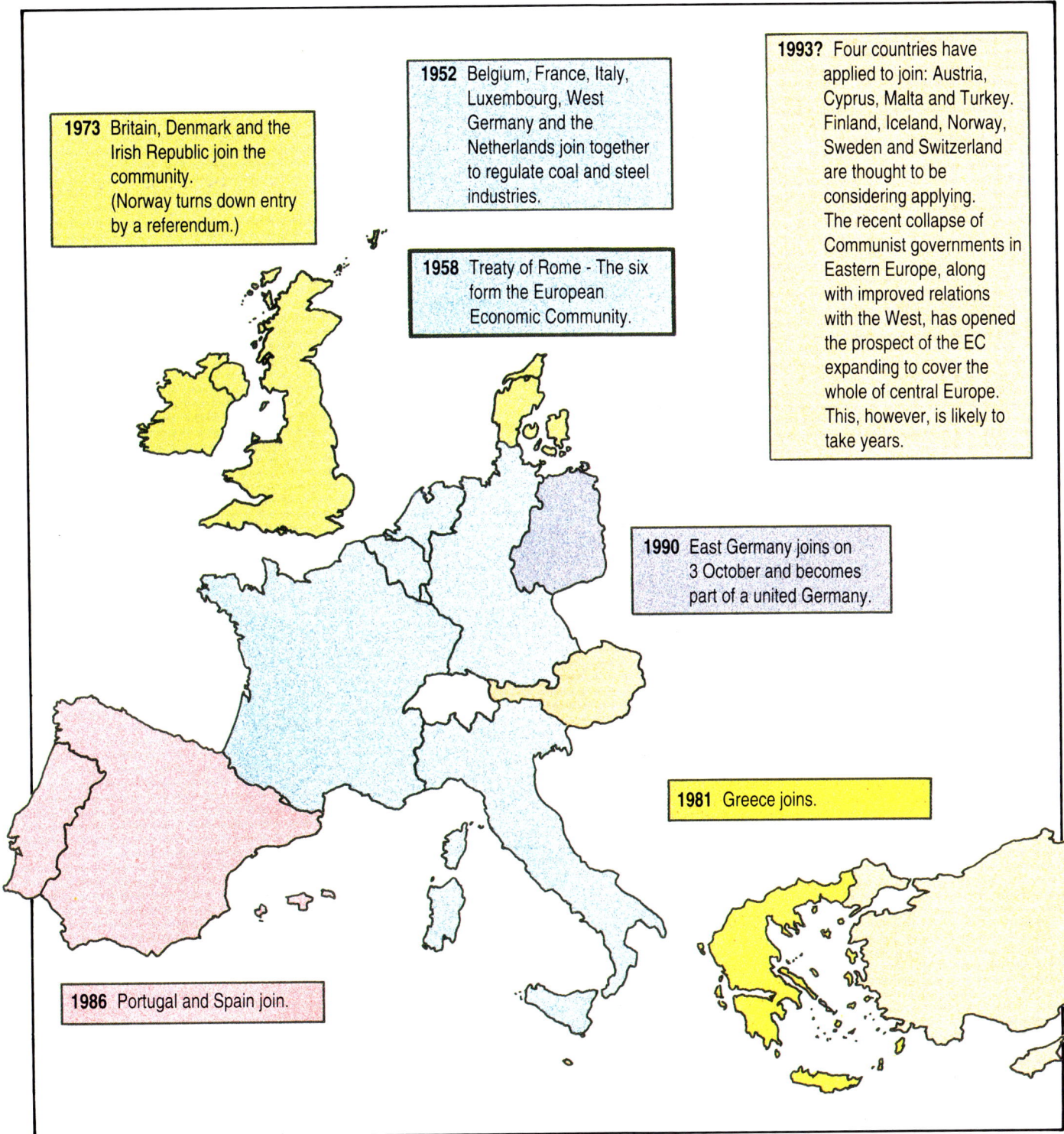

1952 Belgium, France, Italy, Luxembourg, West Germany and the Netherlands join together to regulate coal and steel industries.

1973 Britain, Denmark and the Irish Republic join the community.
(Norway turns down entry by a referendum.)

1958 Treaty of Rome - The six form the European Economic Community.

1993? Four countries have applied to join: Austria, Cyprus, Malta and Turkey. Finland, Iceland, Norway, Sweden and Switzerland are thought to be considering applying. The recent collapse of Communist governments in Eastern Europe, along with improved relations with the West, has opened the prospect of the EC expanding to cover the whole of central Europe. This, however, is likely to take years.

1990 East Germany joins on 3 October and becomes part of a united Germany.

1981 Greece joins.

1986 Portugal and Spain join.

Glossary

AIR TRAFFIC CONTROL (ATC) A computer-aided guidance system for landing aircraft safely.

CABOTAGE Part of the European Community's Single European Market (SEM) laws which allow lorry companies from one country to transport freight in another.

CATALYTIC CONVERTER A device fitted to a car's engine that can remove many of the exhaust gases which pollute the environment.

COMBINED TRANSPORT Forms of transport which use more than one mode per journey; for example, container transport which can be taken by ship, barge, lorry and train.

CONGESTION Overcrowding, as when there are too many cars on the roads.

DEREGULATION Part of the European Community's Single European Market (SEM) laws which encourage competition between transport companies of member states, for example, airlines, by removing laws which keep prices higher than they could be.

EC The European Community (see page 45).

FREIGHT Goods, or merchandise, which are transported from one place to another.

GOLDEN TRIANGLE Europe's industrial backbone, which runs between Glasgow, Frankfurt and Milan.

GREEN TAXATION The scheme whereby car-owners pay more tax on petrol to pay for the damage to the environment caused by pollution from cars.

HAULAGE Freight transported by lorry.

HAULIER A company which hauls freight by road.

HEAVY GOODS VEHICLE (HGV) In the EC, a lorry with a maximum weight of 38 tonnes.

HEAVY RAIL Mainline trains which run between cities.

INFRASTRUCTURE All of the different things that go to make up a transport system. For example, with railways this includes trains, railway lines, electricity, stations, bridges and signalling equipment.

LIGHT RAILWAY A new form of urban rail which has been developed in Germany. Although the trains run on tracks, they can operate alongside roads.

MEMBER STATES Countries which are members of the European Community (EC).

METRO The name for the underground railway in Paris and other cities. Also known as the tube, subway or rapid rail.

NETWORK A connected system. A railway network is made up of all the railway lines in a country or region. A road network is made up of all the roads.

PEDESTRIANIZATION Banning cars from an urban area, so that shoppers can walk around in safety.

PIGGY-BACK TRANSPORT The name for containers carried by rail. Also called a 'rolling motorway'.

RAPID TRANSIT SYSTEM Different forms of urban public transport like buses, trams and trains which together can move large numbers of commuters at speed.

RO-RO Roll-on, roll-off ferries. Vehicles drive on board at one end, and drive off the other at their destination.

RUSH HOUR The peak time in the morning and evening when commuters are going to work or returning home.

SINGLE EUROPEAN MARKET (SEM) The EC's laws which join its member states into one economic unit.

STEVEDORE Person employed to load or unload ships.

TRAINS À GRANDE VITESSE (TGV) France's high-speed trains.

TRANSPORT SYSTEM A particular mode of transport, such as road or rail, including all the bits that go to make it up.

Books to read

There are very few books aimed at teenage readers which look at the complete issue of transport in Europe. It's often a good idea to start by having a look at the index of an encyclopedia.

Transport is frequently discussed in the newspapers. Sometimes the *Financial Times* and *The Economist* do special features on the subject.

Elkington, John, and Julia Hales: Young Green Consumer Guide, (Victor Gollancz, 1990).

Friends of the Earth: An Illustrated Guide to Traffic Calming, (1990).

Mogridge, Martin: Jam Yesterday, Jam Today and Jam Tomorrow, (Transport 2000, 1985). (About road congestion in cities.)

Pannell, J. P. M.: Man the Builder, (Thames and Hudson, 1977).

Ross, Stewart: Towards European Unity, (Wayland, 1989).

Royston, Angela: Just Look at . . . Road Transport, (Macdonald Educational, 1987).

Rutland, Jonathan, and others: Book of Transport, (Ward Lock, 1981).

Sherlock, Harley: Cities are Good for Us, (Transport 2000, 1990).

Transport 2000: The Spring Green Motorway Game, (1990). (A role-play game for pupils about a town facing the effects that a new motorway makes on their lives.)

The easiest statistics to use are 'Vital Travel Statistics' by Stephen Potter and Peter Hughes, Transport 2000, 1990.

Each year the British Government's Department of Transport produces 'Transport Statistics', HMSO. The European Community produces annual transport statistics in 'Europa Transport'. The British Road Federation produces an annual booklet, 'Fact', about road-use.

Further information

British Rail Public Relations
British Railways Board
Euston House
24 Eversholt Street
London NW1 1DZ

CLEAR
(Campaign for Lead-Free Air)
3 Endsleigh Street
London WC1
(For information on lead-free petrol.)

Civil Aviation Authority
CAA House
45-59 Kingsway
London WC1H 0DD

Commission of the European Communities
8 Storey's Gate
London SW1

Department of Transport
2 Marsham Street
London SW1 3EB

Environmental Transport Association
15a George Street
Croydon CR0 1LA

Friends of the Earth
26-28 Underwood Street
London N1 7JQ

International Union of Public Transport
Avenue de l'Uruguay 19
B 10 50 Brussels
Belgium

Transport on Water Association
Engineers Building
No 8 Gate Northside
Royal Victoria Docks
London E16 1BT

Index